reMEMBERSHIP

*New Strategies for Remarkable
Membership Organizations*

kyleSEXTON

REMEMBERSHIP
New Strategies for Remarkable Membership Organizations

Second Edition | ISBN: 978-0-9835703-4-9

Published by IncPlant | Salem, Oregon

Unattributed quotations are by Kyle Sexton
Design and composition by Kyle Sexton
Cover design by Kyle Sexton
Cover Artwork Copyright © iStock by Saul Herrera

For bulk discounts or other resources,
visit www.remembershipbook.com
or call 888-899-8374

~ For Wyatt ~

Great things can happen

when you work hard

on something you love,

for something you love,

because of someone you love.

Contents

Introduction

Networking, and Other Things Not Working

Tell Your Story

Promote Connections Among Members

Joining & Renewals

Pricing & Value

Go

//

Preface

Your organization is unremarkable, therefore no one remarks about you. You keep piling on mediocre features in the hopes one of them will get you across the tipping point.

Your board is discussing relevance, which is a word dangerously close to irrelevance. What follows is a conversation about changing everything and a decision to change nothing.

There you are, lost somewhere between high convenience and high fidelity, just like the post office.

Eighty percent of your members don't show up for anything, yet you still tout participation as the best way to get value from membership. Members will get value when you provide it without requiring their attendance.

You tell businesses that your organization is valuable, yet you don't put a value on it. You give away much and charge little. Will you continue to reward your most time-consuming members (the ones you should have fired) with the lowest membership rates?

You're losing the advantage of proximity. Your members who work next door to each other would rather send an email than meet up for coffee. How will your local association be safe from borderless alternatives?

The tools you need to look as smart as you are have never been more affordable, but your board still says "maybe next year" when it comes to that member-management software investment—the one you've already been putting off for far too long.

Something has gone awry in the world of membership organizations when your members are starting to detach from your association and start their own thing.

If you can't imagine your organization without its sacred cow parade, pageant, or pancake feed, this book is not for you.

If you are not an employee, board member, or high-level volunteer of a chamber of commerce or business-focused association, this book is not for you.

Many of today's membership organizations are living on yesterday's bread while their members drink tomorrow's wine. If your members are putting up with it now, they won't for long.

This book is about renewing your membership-development strategies because your memberships may be worth less than you think.

Introduction

The Safety of Being Mediocre

It used to be that consumers were content to do business however the business wanted it. That's fine if you're a wireless company, where difficult is the norm for the whole industry.

Over the last decade, the banking industry has been waking up to the marketing power of transparency and customization. This is driven largely by competition.

In the association world, your domain is being encroached in nearly every way. Alternatives exist for every feature of membership. *I can replace your marketing benefits with advertising or SEO, no problem. Your chamber of commerce advocacy won't be missed if I use a combination of lobbyists, attorneys, and industry-specific associations.*

As a group, membership organizations are bland. As Seth Godin points out in *Poke the Box*, "You can't get blander than bland."

Marketing guru and publishing game-changer Godin is the author of *Linchpin*, *Tribes*, *The Dip*, and *Purple Cow*, just to name just a few of his seventeen bestsellers.

"We almost never look at merely mediocre products and wonder why they aren't great," writes Godin. "Mediocre services or products do what they're supposed to, but have set the bar so low that it's hardly worth the energy to cross the street to buy them."

Therein lies the problem you face. Unremarkable services from mediocre organizations don't attract fans. When was the last time someone said to you, "You really have to try this vanilla ice cream"? Vanilla is taken. It's been done.

Could it be that you've set the bar at mediocre?

Your vanilla dues model is indefensible. The resulting confusion has infected the rest of the organization, staff included. I remember making up a reason for why my chamber charged dues based on the number of employees: "The impact of our advocacy is greater for larger employers."

But advocacy isn't bought; it's sold. Education and information products and insurance are the same way. The industry must make the case for its relevance by telling its story.

I know exactly what I want from both my wireless company and my government: for them to be relatively invisible utilities.

I know exactly what I want from my insurance company: for it to defend me and protect me if something bad happens.

I know exactly what I want from my car: for it to fire up when I turn the key.

Ask any member what he or she wants from your organization, but don't expect to get an answer. Perhaps this has changed over time. Maybe people used to know what they wanted from you.

Perhaps there just isn't a schema for your association. If there isn't an expectation, it's all too easy to make only the simplest of improvements.

If your organization is a twig in a river's current representing the movement of society, you are flowing along just fine. According to Godin, if you are a rock tumbling along the bottom, you are never going to keep up with the current.

All Systems Go

Tom didn't want to be a bookkeeper. He bought a retail medical supply business and discovered that a sizable chunk of his revenue was tied to Medicare. He was excited about the business-development side of his new venture, not the invoicing.

As we sat together in his makeshift office inside a large storage room, I could tell we had touched on something significant.

"How many hours per week will it take to handle this billing problem?" I asked. "And how much per hour could you generate if you could focus only on business development?"

His estimates:
- Twenty to twenty-five hours per week for bookkeeping
- $200 to $300 in revenue per hour for business development

He hadn't considered outsourcing his bookkeeping problem before. After all, he had been a business owner for just a few weeks. He was still sorting it all out.

"Do you realize it could cost you $208,000 to $390,000 in lost revenue by chasing your Medicare billing challenge yourself?" I inquired.

"You have my attention," Tom replied, his eyes as big as saucers.

"I'm going to take this back to my team and we will provide you with three names," I said. "I recommend that you interview all three of these service providers. Will you do that?"

Not once did we have to discuss membership details. His membership check came three days later. The amount was for double the required dues.

By delivering value before asking for the membership, everybody wins.

All Systems No

Greg supports many community organizations through his business. He's got a growing local chain of restaurants that have the reputation of being fun venues to eat at and rewarding places to work.

Shawna is an enthusiastic membership representative of her regional chamber of commerce. Based on what she told me on the way to our meeting, Greg's membership was a sure thing.

Shawna's impulse was to talk, so her presentation was nothing more than a series of pitches. She had a folder full of brochures and flyers, each representing an event or program she had to tell Greg about.

To this day, Shawna has no idea why Greg isn't a member. She never asked him. Poor Greg got pitched, but what Shawna didn't realize is that presentations like hers are exactly why Greg doesn't like answering his office phone.

More Bad News

Patty Mooney is still fired up. Her husband and business partner, Mark Schulze of Crystal Pyramid, Inc., was a finalist to receive the Most Admired CEO award from the University Club in San Diego. The announcement came a month before the awards ceremony, so Patty and Mark booked a room at Symphony Towers to make the event even more memorable. What an honor it was to be nominated.

They submitted their RSVP for the banquet, and just to be sure, Patty spoke to the banquet organizers during another University Club function and verbally confirmed that she and Mark would be in attendance.

About an hour before the dinner, Patty sought out the organizers to let them know that Mark, one of their nominees, had arrived. According to Patty, "that's when the bomb dropped."

"Oh, you're not on the list," said the organizer. "But don't worry. We'll accommodate you."

Members like to be recognized. They like to be appreciated and acknowledged. So you can imagine how dismayed Mark and Patty were as they sat at what Patty describes as the "kiddy table, like the one in the basement on Thanksgiving Day."

Can we get a do-over on this story?

Clubs that rely on events for contact with their members could—and should—have some parachutes in place just in case the plane starts to sputter.

In this example, one such parachute could be to reserve seats for the staff of the University Club (and their guests) at some of the best tables at the banquet. Another parachute? The organizer could have simply said, "I'm sorry, I'm not finding your table assignment. You two must be at a very special table."

Special indeed. The organizers, whose job it is to make members happy, then quietly do their job by giving up their own seats to Patty and Mark.

I'll never forget this quote from the late Mike McLaran, former CEO of the Salem (Oregon) Area Chamber of Commerce and my mentor for a decade: "If we make a mistake, the affected member hits the jackpot."

At first glance, this approach seems to put the member at the center of the action. But think about it: this philosophy empowers the staffer to deliver some very good news to that member.

Now the staff can feel like Ed McMahon with a big check and a big smile.

Yes, I think a do-over is in order.

It's too bad this club now has less value to Patty and Mark. While the award nomination is still very impressive, their lousy experience will always be the first thing they remember. It could have been different.

The do-over illustrates how organizations with intangible products can create a lasting, tangible impact on their members. Tangible, like the letter Patty wrote to a San Diego magazine about the experience, which eventually made its way to my inbox.

You've heard it before: When people are happy with an experience, they might tell one person. When they are unhappy they tell ten.

Well, maybe that was true in the nineties.

Now it's more like thousands, thanks to virtual friends, social networks, blogs, email lists, list-serves, digital publishing, and an endless list of similar tools.

Networking, and Other Things Not Working

Lessons in Loyalty

"The benefits of a membership association can only be attained and realized if you are an active participant," writes John Rudy, head of Tasty Catering. "The decision to remain a member ultimately depends on the return on investment both from a fiscal and emotional standpoint. Neither can be achieved if you are not an active member."

Fiscal = transactional. Emotional = aspirational. More to come on this important difference.

Tasty Catering's staff is encouraged to attend and participate in meetings so they can decide if a particular association is a good fit for them.

"Our staff has remained loyal to those associations where their contributions are recognized; they have fun and feel as though they are networking with those whom they enjoy, admire, and learn from," he added. If your membership organization is struggling with member retention, I think it's worthwhile to read that statement again.

Rudy made it clear that he only sees a return on investment when his people are involved in a social experience. In my experience, this feeling is over-emphasized in most membership organizations.

Full-Contact Sales

I had the chance to facilitate a focus group at an annual convention of the Association of Chamber of Commerce Executives. This panel consisted of four members of the Greater Raleigh Chamber of Commerce. When I asked how I could position my chamber as a favorable investment for a business owner, two of the panelists responded similarly.

Summarizing: "Don't talk to us about networking. When you say 'networking,' we think 'full-contact sales,' and we don't have time to subject ourselves to salespeople or business owners who are more concerned with selling us something than connecting with us as peers."

John Rudy agrees where his Tasty team is concerned. "Those associations and groups where constant peddling of wares by members occurs are not conducive to growth and are dropped quickly, as it is more about self-serving results than the goals of the group.

"We have terminated memberships in associations when there is a feeling that contributions have been taken advantage of, taken for granted, or ignored," Rudy said. "This has been compounded by groups that are not organized effectively and meetings are haphazard and irregular. Associations with leadership and members who push to achieve personal agendas and financial rewards are other reasons we have decided to not renew memberships in associations."

Avery Horzewski of AVE Consulting agrees. She is a member of Women in Consulting, a San Francisco Bay Area professional organization.

"I really dislike networking and find it uncomfortable," states Horzewski. "But Women in Consulting (WIC) meetings are so unlike any other organization's events that I've attended. From the very beginning, I met other consultants who were willing to answer any questions that I had about running a consulting business.

"Women in Consulting has also provided me with a close group of colleagues whom I can turn to for specific advice, like a board of advisers, really. Whether it's how to handle a sticky client situation, review a client proposal, or offer advice about a new business direction, they're *always* willing to share their insights—and I do the same for them. Many people look at what I do as a very solitary profession—but that's not the case. My WIC colleagues, many of whom are now also good friends, are just that—colleagues."

I'm beginning to believe that networking is a byproduct of getting people together for some other purpose.

Words Mean Things

The difference for Avery is that Women in Consulting is not considered networking. She associates networking with discomfort, just like most of the world's population does. Women in Consulting members are her peers, her friends. I wondered about how Women in Consulting promotes the value of membership, so I poked through their website to find out. As I suspected, the word "networking" is only found in three obscure places on their website. "Network," however, is used in places where you would otherwise find "networking."

A network is something you build, whereas networking is an activity. The gulf between these two words is growing daily. Building a network is something every business must do, but networking is being replaced with advertising or other functions of marketing by many.

Associations that focus on building connections or network development instead of "networking" are not only teaching members how to talk about the organization, but they are also differentiating themselves from the mass of associations that bombard members with "networking opportunities."

People are suspicious of professional networkers. We often feel like we'll be pitched something at some point in the relationship. Professional networkers are sketchy: You're not sure what they do. Perhaps they are job-hoppers, never staying in one place for too long.

Networking is a catch-all term, but I think this word should only apply in cases where people are meeting each other for the first time.

Most chambers of commerce have a morning or evening networking event. These events attract the usual suspects, so networking usually takes a back seat to catching up with friends. After all, why would you choose discomfort over something satisfying? Perhaps events like these aren't really networking after all.

I've been wondering whether *providing networking opportunities* is a noble core function, or just a function of bringing members together for a common purpose. Networking, after all, happens whenever you get a bunch of people in a room.

 Evaluate each of your regularly scheduled events and programs to determine whether they are networking events (meeting new people) or network development (building relationships). If it's network development, stop calling it networking.

Public Speaking, Death, and Networking

Kathleen Watson is a business networking strategist and author of *Net Profit: Business Networking Without the Nerves*. But she's qualified to comment in this area for more reasons than one. Watson's experience with some chambers of commerce wasn't so pleasant.

"At one particular chamber event, I was ignored for over two minutes while trying to enter a conversation," wrote Watson in an email. "At a member orientation for another chamber, one of the chamber ambassadors leaned away from me to whisper something in another veteran member's ear."

I can relate to Kathleen here. Before I came to work for the Salem Area Chamber of Commerce, I was a member of several chambers throughout Oregon. Though most who know me now would find this hard to believe, I am an introvert and become nervous around large groups. I think most people are.

If I hadn't been introduced to other members by one of my co-workers at a chamber function, I would have found it a very intimidating scenario.

On one hand, it's a good thing that your members know each other and enjoy each other's company.

Still, on the other hand, it's regrettable to realize you've got a sizable social gap at your events: those who are new and those who have been around for a while.

The Ambassador program to which Kathleen refers is a popular way for organizations to formalize a system to acclimate new members. It's doubly unfortunate in this case that Kathleen's negative experience comes at the hands of an organizer whose function should have made her more comfortable.

It makes me wonder how many members have been lost by associations for reasons like Kathleen Watson's. I'm sure I'm not the only membership director who has suspected social foul play as a cause for losing a possible long-term member.

Whispers and cold shoulders are kryptonite to grace and hospitality.

"At the only chamber of which I'm still a member," adds Watson, "there's an outstanding mix of friendliness and professionalism. I've been a member of this chamber for nearly ten years. My annual dues are pretty much a no-brainer investment for me."

I'll Have Some Grace with My Membership, Please

The painful experience described by Kathleen Watson calls for an intervention from Shawna Schuh. Shawna is a Certified Speaking Professional and the author of *How to Nail Voice Mail*.

Shawna says if you want to be viewed as gracefully hospitable (rather than stuffy, snobby or cliquish), simply act like the host. Basic, right?

Common sense—and my mother—would tell you to never whisper around other people. Secrets are rude. People's feelings are most often hurt by the worst-case scenario that is playing out in their minds, not by actual events.

If you and your organization foster an environment where whispering is tolerated and cliques are rewarded, your days are numbered. Or, perhaps, you're an invitation-only social club.

That's Not a Membership Organization, or Is It?

United Airlines did a number on me once. After arriving at Portland International Airport more than an hour before my flight was to depart, I watched in awe and angst as a staff of five United Airlines folks took twenty minutes to assist ten people in front of me with their check-in. It was a jumbled mess.

As I swiped my card to check in forty-three minutes before my departure, my reservation could not be retrieved by the automated check-in station, so I politely waited. After a minute or so, I asked for help and was directed to the back of a line of six customers, all waiting to be re-booked by a sole agent.

"I don't need to be re-booked, ma'am," I said. "I just need to be checked in. My flight doesn't leave for another forty minutes."

"You need to wait in that line and our agent will re-book you. I'm not authorized to check you in," she said. Hmm.

Twenty more minutes go by before I get to talk to the agent and she immediately starts to re-book me. "Ma'am," I begged. "My flight doesn't leave for another twenty minutes. Can you just check me in?"

"Sir," she huffed in the most annoyed tone she could manage. I could tell I was about to be lectured. "You should have checked in forty-five minutes before your flight. Why were you late?"

"I wasn't late, ma'am. I got in line an hour before my departure time. Is there any way you can check me in? I really need to be in Los Angeles today."

"You can talk to my supervisor. She's over there." So I went.

I wait for sixty seconds as the supervisor musters up the tolerance to acknowledge my presence. "Yes?" she drones.

"Hello," I said using my sweetest, most not-irritated voice. "Your agent wants to re-book me but I just want to get on my flight. Could you check me in, please?"

"You should've been here forty-five minutes before your flight. Why were you late." (Most questions end in question marks. Hers did not.)

"I stood in this line for an extraordinary amount of time," I explained.

"No, you didn't. Get back in that line and she'll re-book you."

Why do I share this story of United Airlines with you, since they are not a membership organization?

Membership isn't just a business plan; it can also be a service philosophy.

While it's true that I'm not a member of United Airlines in any way, I do feel that I am a member of Delta Airlines. I love Delta. They do all the little things for me that United won't. Delta is nice. They communicate with me in a respectful and kind way at every turn.

I've logged almost 400,000 miles with Delta, and they haven't changed the way they treat me in that entire time. The perks are better, but they aren't any nicer to me because I'm a Silver, Gold, Platinum or Diamond Member.

The day United Airlines made me feel insignificant, I ended up having a pleasant flight on Alaska Airlines. I bought a new one-way ticket for $300, and I'm hoping to get a little satisfaction by including my United Airlines story here.

You could write a book, too, and share your own stories. Perhaps it will be better than therapy. But once an organization does something like this to its own members, there is not enough therapy in the world to remove the bad taste left in members' mouths.

Every day, membership organizations are having tiny "United Airlines moments" with their members. After a while, these moments add up to organizational irrelevance.

Disclaimer: I've had plenty of my own United Airlines moments. Once, I forgot to call back a member of almost thirty years. With my tail between my legs, I went to his office to apologize. When I got there, I instantly knew I was about to talk to an old-school businessman. His desk was a dead giveaway: There was no computer on it, just a phone. The one thing I know about old-school businessmen is that they don't want excuses. He didn't need to remind me that he had been a member for decades, but he did. Of course, he was right to mention it.

My point in sharing this is that you're not always going to get it right. In fact, there will be times when you get it completely wrong with the member who deserves it least.

That was years ago, and we now have a positive and constructive relationship, but only because the spirit in which I approached the situation—and fixed it—mattered.

What Ever Happened to the Original Social Network?

Joe Abraham, author of *Entrepreneurial DNA*, blogs about chambers of commerce in a persistently challenging tone.

"It used to be that I could join a chamber, and it would impact my business," Joe writes. "I would have access to proven education that I could implement in my business. I could meet other business owners and be encouraged through the ups and downs of business. I would have such a positive experience both personally and financially that I would have no choice but to tell every business owner I know about the chamber.

"Question: Are there any fanatical customers left in your chamber of commerce?"

Most associations have a similar challenge ahead of them. With so much competition and online "noise" competing for the same audience, you have a hundred sources where there were once very few.

Health Club Memberships

I spent five years in marketing and advertising for health clubs. I learned that there are two types of sales presentations: museum tours and needs analyses.

The museum tour starts with "Let me show you around," whereas a needs analysis begins by "Why are you here?"

Too many business-focused organizations are giving museum tours of membership features instead of asking the more important questions: "Why are you here?" Or even better: "What's keeping you up at night?" We'll come back to that one.

Health clubs sell memberships, which require that you show up in order to benefit. In my five years, I never had a member who complained about a membership for which they never showed up.

To put it another way, members' expectations for results depend on them coming to the gym, and they accept this responsibility on their part.

The predicament for business associations comes when you realize you've been selling health club memberships to your business association.

Seven Dirty Words for Membership Organizations

Comedian George Carlin had the seven dirty words you can't say on television. I have the seven dirty words you can't say in associations.

You get out what you put in.

Said another way: Return on involvement. You get out of a membership what you put into it. Join, get involved, and your business will grow.

Nothing could be further from the truth.

I hear these phrases in conferences, staff meetings, and board rooms across North America.

The Western Association of Chamber Executives conducted a study, the results of which make up the WACE Toolkit. Sixty-eight percent of respondents indicated they haven't joined the chamber because they don't have time to participate.

They weren't given a sales pitch as part of this study, so why do they think they *have to* participate?

Here's why: participation, as defined by attending meetings and events, is deeply ingrained in the image of associations and chambers of commerce, so much so that it has become the number-one reason for not joining. Regardless of context, this is a problem that needs to be solved.

If your association's core functions include representing the interests of your industry, neighborhood, community, or market sector, then your members have benefited from your existence long before they joined your organization.

The primary value of your organization does not rely on your function—it relies on your purpose. How well you fulfill, communicate, and report on your purpose is another story altogether.

Your functions, events, programs, and initiatives are a secondary reason for joining; however, because they are much easier to promote, they have become your primary selling proposition.

Advocacy is much more difficult to convey. It's more difficult to sell your historical advocacy efforts since you likely weren't there to witness them. This is why effective organizational management becomes more effective the longer it stays in place. There is an exponential increase in performance in the long term when the right team is in place.

Survey Says

Sixty-eight percent of people say they don't have time to participate, but you keep beating that drum. Perhaps you've gained that reputation by rewarding only the people who show up for things. The photos you put in your newsletters and marketing collateral are taken at your events and programs.

Ten percent say they don't join because they don't do business locally. Do they think you are Main Street organizations? Are you? Should you be something more? Answer these questions, then ask your staff and board to answer them as well.

If you decide you are something more, act on it. Be deliberate in every single way. Don't just say that you're a multi-faceted business organization—be one.

For years, you've been teaching your members to drop their membership when what you provide to them works. Maybe you should read that again.

Join the chamber, get involved, and your business will grow. So, they join, they get involved, and their business grows. Then what? If it worked, now they don't have time to participate because they are tending to their growing business, so they drop their membership.

If it works, if membership does what you said it would do, there's nothing more for them. "Thank you, membership organization! It worked, so now I'm leaving. Don't get me wrong; I'm satisfied, I'm just not that loyal."

You have been using guilt to get your members to come to events and programs in order to receive value. That means that each time your members receive an invoice for membership dues, they may feel guilty (all over again) for not taking your advice, for not coming to your meetings, for not being comfortable with networking, for not using the membership the way you teach them they ought to.

You've told them they are not ideal members. They aren't your favorites. You reward the ones who come to meetings, and that's all. The only photos you promote are ones taken at your events and all of them feature the cool kids.

Membership Drive Intervention

Years ago, I wrote an open letter to chambers of commerce who were burning through volunteers and churning through members with membership drives. I wasn't the first to talk about it, but I still run into people who tell me they pass my letter around to staff and board members. I hear it's even posted in break rooms.

Dear Chamber of Commerce,

It's because I love you that I write this letter. Please give up membership drives. I understand how a chamber could get addicted to membership driving, so

I'm not judging you. When your chamber needs that kick, and your budget counts on it, the rush of members going through your system can feel so great!

But the lows are low. When you need another hit of members and you've already smoked them all, where do you go? Another membership drive? Do you call your doctor and get the patch?

Quitting cold turkey seems a daunting task. If you don't find something else soon, you're going to start driving again and it's a downward spiral from there.

So now you're up to two drives a year to feed your habit. Members stop referring year round because they are waiting for a drive. Those referrals were like endorphins to your nervous system. Now there are basically two times per year that you get to feel the high of new members running through your system.

Your addiction to new members will eventually cause your volunteers to organize an intervention. "We're tired of calling on businesses twice a year," they say. "And we feel like we don't even know you anymore." A wedge has been driven between you.

"We just want our membership director back," they plead. "The one we loved before all of the membership driving began." They're hoping you won't turn to violence... or worse, a fundraising consultant.

Let's not even get into all of the enablers... The codependency runs deep into your board and CEO. They look the other way in order to have the dollars in the bank, and they aren't helping a bit. Your treasurer will not show up for the intervention.

What if you could replace the nicotine of membership drives with the endorphins of an ongoing referral system? It would be like replacing smoking with jogging. The benefits to the health of your organization would be tremendous.

Imagine, no more massive exodus from your membership upon the first-year anniversary. No more calling on a prospect only to be turned away with "I tried it a few years ago and I didn't get any service, so I dropped it."

What if you were to bring on new members at a pace that could gain you a better relationship with them, instead of just a turn-and-burn? I bet you'd get more dollars per member per year. I bet your average length of membership would increase over time. And I bet you'd be perceived as an engaging organization that's doing great things without the cloud of a pressured referral-sales organization.

Quitting Membership Drives Now Greatly Reduces Serious Risks to Your Chamber's Health.

There are only three conditions under which I could endorse a membership drive:

1. Have a proven system for *successfully* on-boarding masses of members. This means your first-year retention rate is within twenty percent of your overall retention rate.

2. Know (to the penny) your variable cost per membership.
3. Count people as members only after they renew on their own. Up to this point, they can be treated as trial members.

Even following these criteria, few markets can endure annual—or even biannual—campaigns.

Have-to, Ought-to, Want-to

If you've ever conducted a cattle-call for your association in the form of a membership drive, you've probably also noticed that your association loses a greater percentage of new members gained during membership drives than those gained during any other time of the year.

This is because your organization didn't adjust its member orientation, training, and acclimation processes accordingly.

Keith Woods, CEO of the North Coast Builders Exchange and former CEO of the Santa Rosa (CA) Chamber of Commerce, is a popular speaker and has worked for decades as a trainer for membership associations. Woods says members fall into one of three distinct categories:

- Have-to
- Ought-to
- Want-to

When you run a membership drive, or your incoming board president calls on someone to join your association, Have-tos join your organization. You've got their money. Fine.

But play this out with me. Someone walks into a Have-to's business and says, "I see from the plaque on the wall that you're a member of the chamber of commerce."

The Have-to shrugs her shoulders, rolls her eyes a little, and says, "I had to." This is a drag on your brand.

The Ought-tos joined long ago. They get what you do and why you do it. They appreciate your organization, even though they admit they aren't familiar with the depth of your function. They renew quietly each year. Depending on the age of your organization, you need these members.

Side note: I believe Ought-tos aren't membership prospects for most associations anymore, especially chambers of commerce.

Ought-to members represent what I call "Legacy Businesses." They are deeply entrenched in their network or industry. They don't pay any mind to social media trends and might still have their first website from 1999 up and running. They are more interested in sun-setting than reinventing. They may be a professional services firm or a manufacturing conglomerate. Perhaps they still advertise in the

Yellow Pages, but it's just to reassure people that they are still in business.

The Want-to might be your ideal member and may just represent the future of your membership development efforts. The Want-to is actively seeking solutions to his or her business challenges.

But you've been scaring away Want-tos for years. You haven't trained them on the pathways to follow in order to achieve their business goals.

You've used voodoo codes and secret handshakes to create a rumor mill around how to do business with you.

The lost opportunity for revenue with this crowd pales in comparison to the lost opportunity for engagement. These are the active members who want to love you if you'll just let them.

Be easy to work with. Have pricing and packaging that reflects your strengths and flexibility. Be open to their involvement from the get-go and don't make them sit through a waiting period. Connect them to their peers in your organization and reassure them right away that they are in the right place.

You teach people how to treat you. You also teach the people you want to do business with. Nurturing the Want-to member will attract more of the same. Numerous organizations do door-to-door cold calling instead of asking their bread-and-butter members a simple question: "What can we do to be more valuable to you?"

Building a better mousetrap means designing your system around the member instead of around your staff or internal protocol.

Don't ask the people holding shovels how many elephants should be in the parade.

Tell Your Story

You Don't Function in Isolation

A chamber of commerce will qualify its ability to measure against other organizations by whether or not it acts as a convention and visitors' bureau or as the economic development arm of the city.

Who cares? Turf is a nasty thing. It's usually paired with ego and politics. If you are a chamber of commerce, you produce what the economic development corporation (EDC) sells. And even if someone else serves as your community's convention and visitors' bureau (CVB), your organization produces what the CVB sells.

Maura Gast, executive director of the Irving, Texas, Convention & Visitors Bureau puts this into perfect perspective:

"If you build a place where people want to visit, you build a place where people want to live. If you build a place where people want to live, you build a place where people want to work. If you build a place where people want to work, you build a place where business needs to be. And if you build a place where business has to be, you'll build a place where people have to visit."

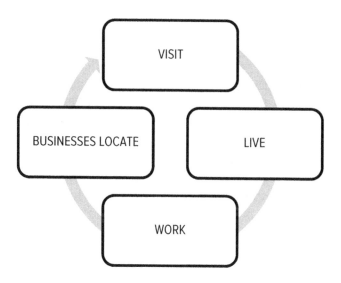

During a visit to Santa Rosa, California, I was invited to dinner at John Ash & Co., a legendary restaurant located at the beautiful Vintner's Inn. That night, the restaurant had a second menu, which was part of a county-wide promotion called Restaurant Week. More than a hundred restaurants across Sonoma County offered a three-course dinner for $19, $29, or $39.

Turns out, it wasn't the Santa Rosa CVB or Chamber of Commerce that ran this promotion; it was the Sonoma County Economic Development Board. To me, this was a sign that Sonoma County has starters in the right places. I know of a thousand regions where Restaurant Week would have been sabotaged or resented because it encroaches on someone else's turf. That's just not right.

Gast's comment forces you to consider the partners involved in your endeavors. For chambers of commerce, CVBs, and EDCs, the relationship is pretty clear: to foster or create competition among regional organizations is to undermine their relationships.

Instead of getting permission, start something. It sure would be nice to break out of this "turf" thing. Create a culture of innovation in your region, industry, or organization by granting permission to start things. Innovate.

Mission, Vision, and Function

A much more challenging membership-based business organization might be one like the International Hotel & Restaurant Association (IH&RA). Their members are mostly national hotel and restaurant associations.

Confused yet? Their members have members of their own. To further complicate the issue, their members do not have the luxury of having locality, demography, geography, or even language in common with each other. The function of an organization like IH&RA is complicated by these issues.

On the other hand, according to the Western Association of Chamber Executives, the core functions of a chamber of commerce are pretty straightforward:
- Strengthen the local economy

- Represent business interests in government
- Take political action and develop leaders
- Promote the community
- Provide networking opportunities

Has your membership organization determined your core functions?

Different from your mission statement, vision statement, or unique selling proposition, your core functions represent how your members—and the public—will measure your performance.

Think of your association as a college course. What would be contained in your syllabus? If there are definable stages in the business life of your members, how many syllabi will it take to cover your core functions?

Chambers of commerce usually have five core functions, but some also serve a tourism function in their city or town. That could be covered under "promoting the community" for obvious reasons, but tourism is probably more appropriately labeled as "strengthening the local economy."

Engage Members Through Communication (Without Asking Them to Show Up)

It was about a decade ago when I got fed up (the first time) with satisfied members cancelling their memberships by writing "no time to participate" on their returned invoices. I pinned the notes on my bulletin board, deciding to save them until I could figure out what I was going to do about the problem.

These members were plenty satisfied, but not loyal. On their invoices, some would write thank-you notes.

"Thanks for all you do! I'm pleased with your service, but I no longer have time to participate."

*"No time to participate"
isn't just a reason to
cancel a membership;
it's an escape from
the guilt and punishment
you've been issuing as your
members focus on other
priorities.*

What is the difference, then, between satisfaction and loyalty? Loyalty is passing up a momentarily better option and instead staying with you. Is doing nothing, then, the better option?

It seems that many chambers of commerce and associations are issuing guilt via mail and email on a regular basis. And we've also been failing to teach members what comes next, no matter the stage of business or membership.

Join, use our benefits, and then you won't have time to come to our events and meetings anymore, all because our benefits worked. So what's next?

Your membership organization needs a new narrative. I call mine Pathways. When I ask members for one word to describe why they join and stay, they mostly answer advocacy for business, involvement in the community, or marketing and visibility. I'm not one for acronyms, but that spells A.I.M.

If your main objective is to support advocacy, you can ignore everything under marketing and involvement. If you want involvement in the community, you can ignore everything under advocacy and marketing.

You get the pattern, but don't get ahead of yourself: If your main goal is marketing, your members might still feel that you cannot ignore the aspects of community involvement, and this makes sense. The best marketing is going to have some components of community involvement.

There is a culture among many organizations that requires "getting involved" if you want members to get their money's worth. Your most involved members are sometimes also the loudest on this point. "You can't join without getting involved," they'll say. Or "You get out what you put in."

Not true.

Your board and staff can start a new campaign: "You never even have to lift a finger to participate in our activities to get value from your membership."

I'll never forget when we heard our board chair repeat this in an address to the membership. (Cue happy dance.)

The Fine Line Between Satisfaction and Loyalty

It can be truly confusing to receive cancellation notices like this one: "You've done a terrific job, and I'm not dissatisfied in any way, but I won't be renewing my membership this year."

It's tempting to skirt the issue by removing annual renewals from your organization. Switching to invisible, low, automatic monthly payments seems like a brilliant idea.

Health clubs have been doing business this way since the 80s, you think to yourself. IHRSA, the International Health, Racquet & Sportsclub

Association, reports health clubs have an average membership retention rate of seventy-five percent. If this rate were higher, I could support this argument, but most associations have average retention rates higher than this.

So we're left to grapple with this issue of member loyalty without resorting to trickery or invisible payment mechanisms.

In his book *Permission Marketing*, Seth Godin says we must turn strangers into friends, friends into customers, and customers into loyal customers.

I recently re-read *Permission Marketing* to see if his prediction of the future of marketing was still on point, given the social media movement that is still in full force as I write this. In 1999, the burning issue Godin addressed was specific to email and website marketing. Godin is brilliant, and *Permission Marketing* is still important. I suspect that is why he has never rewritten it.

When you visit a website and it asks you to enter your name and email address to access specific information or receive an electronic newsletter, this is permission marketing. You are giving the publisher permission to market to you.

Social media is similar. When people like your business on Facebook or follow you on Twitter, they are giving you permission to market to them. It's a different kind of marketing than what they want, however.

Here are the top ten reasons consumers follow a company on social media, according to research reported by *Social Media Today*:

- Forty percent want to receive discounts and promotions
- Thirty-seven percent want to show their support for the brand/company to others
- Thirty-six percent want get free samples or coupons
- Thirty-four percent want to stay informed about the activities of the company
- Thirty-three percent want to get updates on future products
- Thirty percent want to get updates and information on future sales
- Twenty-seven percent like to get fun and entertainment out of following a business online
- Twenty-five percent want to get access to exclusive content
- Twenty-two percent mentioned they were referred by someone to follow this brand/company
- Twenty-one percent just want to learn more about the company

The purpose of permission marketing is to turn strangers into friends. This is the first critical conversion. Based on the top ten reasons consumers follow you on social media, calling your followers "fans" would be a stretch.

True loyalty is internal, not external. I don't think that just because your wireless company makes it difficult to switch to another carrier, your continued business with them can be interpreted as loyalty. Similarly, your health club's two-year agreement and relatively quiet collection of dues from your bank account cannot be interpreted as loyalty.

Another note on Godin: You could read *Tribes* and replace the word "tribe" with the name of your association in almost every instance. Read it, and then read it again because he makes some points in a manner more elegant than simple.

*"Loyalty
is what we call
it when someone
refuses a momentarily
better option."
~ Seth Godin*

Attention Problem

My father's snow blower allows him to get safely from his cabin to his truck, but he used to use a shovel on the hundred-foot walkway on his high desert property.

Imagine the surprise we'd have if we happened upon ol' Dad pushing his snow blower—without any fuel—and still expecting the walkway to clear. We would know for certain that Dad had lost his mind.

Here is this great piece of technology that does in minutes what used to take hours—but there's no fuel in the tank. Ineffective. Illogical. Inoperable.

Your communications need fuel just like the snow blower does. Emails, headlines, and homepages have run out of fuel, yet you expect the same result.

You have an attention problem that causes your organization to send too many emails. You've known for years that your communications have become less effective, but you don't have an alternative.

The problem is that attention is more valuable than money. Money comes and goes. You can blow a few bucks and go make more money. You can lose a member's renewal and get him or her back months or years later.

Attention, though, is precious. Once you lose someone's attention, you've certainly lost their money forever. Every time you send an email, you're using a metaphorical exclamation point.

God has given each of us a limited number of exclamation points to use in our entire lifetime. Once you have used them all, you are un-friended, un-followed, un-liked, un-fanned, muted, deleted, marked as spam, and banned permanently.

Here are seven ways organizations waste the attention of their audiences.

Talking about events. Statistics show that an average of twenty percent of your members will attend events and programs regularly this year. Your efforts to convert the other eighty percent are costing you valuable attention through membership churn, unsubscribes, and reduced open rates.

Repetitive content and last-chance notifications. What's one more email? Your members must have not received the other three announcements. The staff person sending the last-chance notification is accountable for the attendance at the meeting, not the rate at which future emails are read. You teach people how to treat you, and this behavior teaches your members that you will nag them until they take action—or stop reading your emails entirely.

Pitching. It's the reason we're always "just looking" at the car dealership and the reason we roll our eyes when we hear the doorbell ring. Pitching is cheap, lazy, and disrespectful—a fishing expedition. It talks more than listens and ignores a prospects' objections. Spam is a pitch.

Starting meetings late. Nothing rewards the tardy and punishes the on time more than starting the meeting late. Stop rewarding bad behavior.

Using the whole hour. Just because the calendar said the meeting would last an hour, there is no reason to force it. When was the last time you gave someone the gift of time? Get through the agenda and cut everyone loose.

Lack of segmentation. You've failed to use the knowledge of your members to make your organization smarter. Your members have told you they aren't interested in attending your events... by not attending your events. They would have subscribed to your government affairs email list if you had given them the option, but you send everything to everyone because it's all so important.

Selling access to your list. Much of the digital marketing industry calls this practice spam. Ah, but you're addicted to that money. And you've got a line of members wanting to pay you to send their spam for them. They would do it themselves, but no one will sign up for their mailing list because, well... because they don't want to get spammed.

So what is the remedy?

1. Segment your list according to what you know about your members.
2. Allow members to choose their own interests, even if it's none.
3. Tell stories. Use examples. Make someone else famous. Spend your exclamation points to share how others demonstrate your organization's values.

4. Generate interest with a bit of mystery. Obvious is weak, subtle is power.
5. If you have to keep sending other people's spam, take your name off of it. And your logo. And your email address. It keeps your members from reading the emails you actually want them to see and reinforces the association between spam and your .org or .com domain. Turn that e-blast (a euphemism for spam) into a separate media business (owned by your organization) with a separate domain and a separate email address. This allows you to open up your e-blasts to non-member subscriptions and grow your audience organically.

The Referral Age Has Replaced the Information Age

Information is no longer a membership benefit. The proliferation of stats and facts is not exclusive to your organization. It's out there, somewhere.

In a time when search engines correct your spelling and intuitively suggest other search terms to provide more accurate results, it's safe to say that information is everywhere, and people don't care where it comes from.

People would rather take the recommendation of a complete stranger than conduct their own due diligence based on available information.

Because of this, the most effective communications strategies include creating your own content and adding a filter, or perspective, to other current news and information.

Advertising Age does a terrific job of this. After all, think about its audience. Folks who are successful in the business of creating advertisements for an increasingly attention-deprived world probably have a little A.D.D. themselves. *Advertising Age* has to be good at what it does.

By the time I receive my *Advertising Age* magazine in the mail, I've already seen most of the articles from my email subscriptions. The *Advertising Age* team has divided up the entire magazine into different interest areas and sends them out electronically in a timelier fashion.

But we don't mind seeing content a second time when it is in a different format. We have different expectations of digital communications. They must be timely if they are to be relevant.

Your membership organization likely has a print newsletter and (various) emails. Your newsletter may already contain the makings for several e-publications for segmented audiences among your members.

An aside on electronic communications: If you suspect you are sending out too many emails to your members, you probably are. If you wonder about how many of your emails are getting read, you'll be appalled at how many are even being opened.

If you haven't been enforcing a policy for your staff about the frequency of sending emails—or worse, you don't even have a policy—you may have already lost the opportunity to communicate with your members via email.

Fix it now. No more than one email a week. Start with the Rule of Sixes and evolve from there: No more than six items per email, no more than six lines per item, and no more than six words per headline. If you can't say it in six lines, include a link to your website.

Keep it concise. Never repeat the same article from a previous week. Resist the urge to send out a mass email for a special purpose that provides value only to you. Use targeted or special-interest lists for this instead.

Segmenting your communications seems like a daunting task, but your relevance depends on it. It could be that by subjecting your members to content they're not interested in, you've turned them off already.

If a member has told you (in words or actions) that he or she is not interested in attending events, the event-heavy promotional messages in your electronic communications may as well read, "We don't want you as a member if you don't come to our events."

Communicating in an Advertising Age

How would *Advertising Age* overhaul your communications? Let's say your print newsletter contains:

- A feature story
- Your upcoming events
- A column from the CEO
- Industry or advocacy update
- A column from the board chair
- News from members
- Events from members
- Timely stats and trends

Segment 1: *Insights* contains the columns from your CEO and board chair, plus timely stats and trends.

Segment 2: *E-vents* features your events, plus upcoming events submitted by members.

Segment 3: *Newsroom* includes news items (not events) submitted by members.

Segment 4: *Insider* includes only the industry or advocacy work of your organization.

If you've been keeping track, the only part of your print newsletter not included in your new email segments is the cover story, which provides value to those who want to spend time with your printed publication.

The hard part will be allowing members to pick and choose which e-publications they want without your interference. Perhaps the hardest part will be sending out these e-pubs before your print newsletter hits mailboxes.

Forcing publications on members is a disservice, not a membership benefit.

Remarkable membership organizations have the confidence to let the member choose —and control— the information they want to receive from you.

Teach Members How to Talk About You

When an organization says it has a membership-retention problem, it may actually have a sales problem. People attach emotion and expectation to joining an association. Will my competition be there? Will people be friendly? Will I have something to contribute?

I've been teaching branding strategies to businesses and non-profits for fifteen years, but the following simple statement from Vice President and Head of Strategy Eric Alper of Sid Lee, a Montreal-based creative services firm, almost eliminates the need for lessons:

*"If you don't tell your story,
the public will make up
one about you."*

~ Eric Alper

The instruction behind the statement is shockingly simple: tell your story.

It's not "Keep advertising on price and tell a story" or "Come up with a clever slogan and a story." Just *tell your story*.

I find that most membership organizations don't tell their stories very well. Scratch that: I find that *most organizations* don't tell their stories well, regardless of business model or tax status.

When the message is clear, the money comes easy. If you are a business-focused membership organization, are your members not your product? If members benefit from your services, do they not become your story?

Perhaps your story is better told by your members.

Stories: Humanity in Your Brand

Tom's Shoes puts great stories of charity into a box of shoes and mails them to you for money. Go to Toms.com and see for yourself.

Burt's Bees sells saving the earth, as well as my favorite lip balm. It's too bad membership organizations don't produce anything. Or do they?

Your members' joyful loyalty is your product. The unique attributes of your members' stories become your story. Their fears are yours. Their opportunities are shared by all in your organization. They're your common ground.

Years ago, a member of the Salem Area Chamber of Commerce asked us to help her tell her story. The result was a couple of thirty-second television commercials in which two different company spokespeople told the story of why they give to causes that benefit teachers and students in the classroom. The emotional impact of these stories was great. I remember saying, "If this process didn't cost almost $4,000, we'd do more of them."

The cost of video has gone down so much that I've had to follow through on that statement.

With my trusty digital HD video camera (which costs around a hundred bucks), a lavaliere microphone, some halogen work lights from the hardware store, and a $300 video editor (I use Camtasia Studio), I produce stories that humanize my organization. Picture a video testimonial shot in the style of your favorite interview from *60 Minutes*.

In the end, your viewers may wonder if you're promoting yourself or your members. Perfect.

Telling Your Story with Video

If you don't tell your story, the public will make up a story about you. This is a painful realization because myths are more powerful than fact. Once someone has made up a story about you, their story is difficult to overcome. Consumers don't like to be told they are wrong.

A decade ago, I was in a room full of membership directors and executives wishing aloud for a marketing budget that would allow them to afford video. Today, YouTube is free, and any smart phone purchased since 2012 comes equipped with an HD video camera. But you still haven't told your story on video, so we know it's not about the budget. You just don't have a compelling story to tell.

How do we tell our stories in a way that attracts the right members, repels the wrong members, and turns strangers into friends?

Here's a winning formula I've used for years: rather than talk about what you do, showcase those you serve. Simple, right?

Your members are your product, so talk about them. Talk about their values and dreams: dreams are emotional, and values transfer to your organization.

This same philosophy has been featured by thought leader Gary Vaynerchuk in his best-selling book, *Jab, Jab, Jab, Right Hook—How to Tell Your Story in a Noisy Social World*. Tell a story (jab), give something for free (jab), or share a tip (jab), and then try to sell the audience on your brand (right hook).

Vaynerchuk's title gives a roadmap to balancing valuable content with promotion through video and other media.

Carmine Gallo, in his book *Talk Like TED*, points out that early footage of Steve Jobs, eventually renowned for his stage presence, shows a very anxious young speaker. No doubt you and your members will feel anxious on camera in the beginning, too. Here are some strategies to help you feel more comfortable in front of the camera.

1. Film your practice sessions and watch them fully.
2. Observe how others perform on camera. Are they looking at the camera or are they being interviewed by someone off screen? Which do you think looks better?
3. Turn your laptop into a teleprompter by downloading free teleprompter software. Position the teleprompter behind and above the camera, or, if you prefer the interview format—like something you'd see on *Dateline* or *20/20*—place the teleprompter at a five-degree angle to the right or left of the camera.

The single biggest marketing impact your organization can make is to make someone famous. Talking about those you serve is a more effective long-term storytelling strategy. Here are the eleven criteria I've used in choosing members to make famous:

1. They must love their community.
2. They must have a consumer focus (rather than business-to-business) to engage a broader audience.
3. They must love their community.

4. Their businesses must be locally owned—no big boxes.
5. They must love their community.
6. Their businesses must be owner operated so anyone can drop by and meet the owner.
7. They must love their community.
8. Their businesses cannot be franchises or parts of a national network.
9. They must love their community.
10. They must be off the beaten path.
11. They must love their community.

You're picking favorites, just like a magazine editor would. If you're like most membership organizations, picking a favorite goes against the grain of your culture, but this exercise isn't part of your member services; it's marketing through storytelling.

After selecting members to feature according to your criteria, you need to get your material ready. I like to ask a few questions and talking points to get my subjects comfortable on camera:

- Tell me about your first job.
- If you had an evil twin, what would his/her name be?
- How is it that you came to own this business?

From there, a fifteen-minute interview will give you plenty of content for a two- to three-minute finished product.

When the message is clear, the money comes easy.

Promote Connections Among Members

Peer Communities Provide Member Value

One of the key values of a membership organization is a sense of community. Contrary to how most organizations function, this doesn't mean gathering everyone in the same room.

For decades, you've gone to great lengths to treat all members the same, and your financials are getting beaten up for it.

One simple way your membership organization can create value is to leverage your experience in networking and special events to create exclusive connection events for members.

Your members are unique, and they want to be treated that way. Business owners want to connect with their peers, not be sold to. Value is in the eyes of the member.

Young Professionals programs are now common associations and have varying degrees of impact. I recently aged out of the young professionals program I co-founded a decade ago and now see the mistake.

It's ironic, I know, to now realize that in an effort to create a sense of community, we kicked people out just as they were finding their place in the community.

The National Speakers Association has a better model. They build a group around generations. Rather than aging out at forty, the group stays together because their group, NSA/XY, is based on birth year instead of age.

**By segmenting
your membership
and promoting connections
within common segments
among your tribe,
you avoid becoming
a subscription.**

Participation versus Partnership

The membership business model tends to undervalue individual benefits because most functions of the organization are included in a package. For items that aren't included, the assumption is that you'll have reduced rates for members, whereas non-members pay retail rates.

Too often, when new features of membership are added, they are essentially given away. The thinking here is that these one or two new benefits will attract enough new members to justify giving them away to all.

This is a race to the bottom, and I bet you'll get there. If this describes your membership organization, you're not alone.

Event-related benefits provide an experience for participants and generally lend a different flavor to your brand. There's a culture at each event that arises based on who is there, and it may be different than the culture at the last event.

The success of your mixers depends on whether your event is peer-to-peer or shark-to-prey.

The popularity of your gala event will depend on the quality of the food and the overall "fun factor."

And the brand of your organization will depend on whether your members attend events because they feel they are productive and meaningful, or because they feel guilty about missing them.

Guilt is a funny thing. Many associations are good at guilt. If you think you're not, let's make sure.

If you've ever said, "You get out of our association what you put into it," you may be good at guilt.

If you've ever said, "Join, get involved, and your business will grow," you may be good at guilt.

If you've ever told someone, "I haven't seen you at any meetings lately," then you're *pretty good* at guilt.

The problem isn't that you're really good at events; it's your assumption that what is valuable to *you* will be valuable to *them*. Your membership organization's value is subjective.

In your race to the bottom, you've added membership benefits that serve the squeaky wheels. You may have artificially inflated the value of showing up for events at a time when your competition is building remarkable programs, not more programs.

Your competition includes alternatives such as networking groups, Little League, and charitable organizations. Any functions of your target-members' lives that they love more than you are competition.

What if you're
just not that
remarkable?
You are replaceable,
probably upon renewal.

Are you prepared for every single member to show up for your event? If not, stop inviting everyone. The days of the cattle call are long gone.

If your organization exists for the advocacy of business, industry, or social cause, align your features and functions accordingly.

Get Something, or Get Something Done

Mick Fleming is the president and CEO of the Association of Chamber of Commerce Executives, a professional association for chamber professionals, and has been in the association business for a few decades. Mick suggests there are two types of members in an organization: "Those who want to get something, and those who want to get something done."

I find that there is a difference in longevity among members who simply want to get something from you and those who want to get something done. In the case of the former, once they get what they're looking for, they are more inclined to leave. Mission accomplished.

If you don't engage them with features of your organization that will entice them to stick around and *get something more* or *get something done*, you may lose them.

Until now, there hasn't been a map for this.

Four Business Profiles

Now, you've been introduced to two different concepts I've been talking about for years: *participation versus partnership* and *get something or get something done.*

If we take an academic approach to these concepts, they fit together nicely in a classic two-by-two matrix.

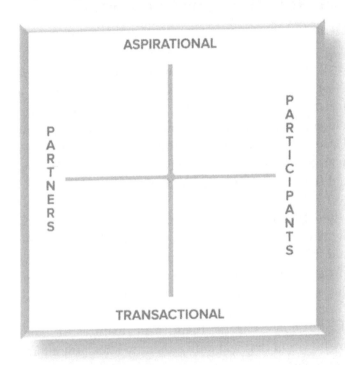

Some want to be involved; some don't. Some have to get something *from* their membership; others want to get something done *through* your organization. Combinations of these traits provide a matrix to help your organization find values for four distinctly different member profiles.

When you look over your membership programming, are you serving each of the four member profiles? Do you provide value for members in each of these four quadrants?

The Greater Kitchener-Waterloo Chamber of Commerce took these concepts even further with their matrix and gave each quadrant a name and traits. When it was shared with me, I applied my twenty years in membership to it and took it even further.

Transactional participants (the bottom right) want to sell their stuff to everyone. Transactional partners (the bottom left) want you to bring the benefits of membership to their place of business because they don't feel they can leave. Next we've got aspirational participants (the top right)—if they're not buying tables of eight at your events, they're sponsoring them. Finally, aspirational partners (the top left) are stakeholders who would rather perform a task for you than be on your board.

When using this format to consider what your members want from you, it becomes clear that you're not running a membership organization; you're running *four different* membership organizations. The sense of community that glues your members to your organization—and to each other—is more exclusive than you previously thought.

All members are invested partners when they write out checks for their membership dues. But there are different levels of involvement. There's your own interpretation of what involvement looks like (from an organizational standpoint), but ultimately it's up to each member (participant) to determine what involvement means.

If you're defining "involvement" in terms of how many people show up for meetings and events, keep in mind that your members are measuring it differently than you are.

For example, when your members respond to an online survey, poll, or questionnaire, they believe they've just volunteered for you. They consider providing feedback involvement.

Going back to the matrix, let's look at the top and bottom halves. The bottom has transactional members, and the top has aspirational members. These are folks who are part of your organization because they get what you do, they're glad that you do it, and, most of all, they're glad that they don't have to do it themselves.

Combinations of these axis points create four distinctly different member profiles.

Bottom Right: the Business Builder
- Needs the most
- Has more time than money
- Considers showing up important

- Free marketing opportunities
- Is price conscious
- Volunteers for activities
- Wants educational programs

Typical individuals found in the Business Builder quadrant:
- Small office/home office business owners
- Independent sales representatives
- Multi-level marketing representatives
- Real estate agents
- Salespeople
- Charities
- Retired individuals

Bottom Left: the Business Investor
- Wants you to bring the benefits to them
- Is less likely to show up to events
- Is happy to host an event
- Is value conscious
- May participate in affinity programs
- Wants promotion
- Is willing to pay for advertising

Typical businesses found in the Business Investor quadrant:
- Main Street businesses
- Restaurants and retail
- Hotels and conference centers
- Entertainment/music venues
- Sporting event venues
- Art museums

Top Right: the Community Builder

- Attends idea summits
- Is interested in public policy efforts
- Is interested in committees and task forces
- Is interested in group volunteer activities
- Is interested in team building
- Is interested in leadership development
- Is interested in sponsoring events or programs

Typical businesses found in the Community Builder quadrant:
- Banks and credit unions
- Title and escrow companies
- Real estate development firms
- Commercial real estate brokerages
- Business law firms
- Accounting firms
- Insurance companies
- Engineering firms
- Architecture firms
- Software firms

Top Left: the Community Investor
- Is a stakeholder in the region
- Appreciates that you take political action
- Interested in tasks, not committees
- Enjoys golf and gala events
- Has least amount of free time
- Keeps hands clean
- Never mixes with Business Builders

Typical businesses found in the Community Investor quadrant:
- Large-employer businesses

- Hospitals
- Universities
- Municipalities
- Multi-business entrepreneurs
- Utility companies

As I've mentioned before, here's where I see a lot of membership organizations make a big mistake: They only convey their value to members in terms of showing up. They say the dreaded phrase "You only get out of it what you put into it."

I am here to tell you that you're wrong about that. You get out so much more than you could ever put into it. You have to be able to convey your value in a way that says, "If you only write a check for membership, you get these things—even without showing up."

Create a pathway for people. Their memberships are going to help them reach their business goals, and when they do, the time they previously spent working with your organization on achieving those goals time is going to need to be replaced with some other visibility at some point.

 Create a pathway for each of the three membership goals referenced on page forty-four: advocacy and access, involvement in the community, and marketing (A.I.M.). Once they have identified their goal, what benefits of membership should they tune in to? What can they ignore?

At some point, every membership organization needs to create a pathway for its members to follow:

Join our organization. If you want to get involved, then do that. It's going to work, and when it works, we've got a different membership for you. Here are examples of members who used to be involved in a lot of things and now they're not because those things worked. Now they're managing their growing businesses and attend our events less frequently. And that's okay.

Joining & Renewals

A-B-Cs of Membership

A members are ideal. They come around once in a blue moon. They're easy to work with, but they also push you to do remarkable work. Sometimes, they ask for something that isn't on your regular menu.

B members are your bread and butter. These are the folks that you see every day. They're the ones who keep the lights on and the staff paid. They are profitable to your organization, and amazed by you.

C members are the ones who your organization perhaps ought to fire. These folks don't pay for themselves, financially. I like to call them the cusstomers because they make you pull your hair out and cuss. I know that sounds kind of harsh, but if you consider the amount of energy they drain from your organization, it isn't harsh enough. The cuss-tomer is taking away precious time and resources, both of which are better invested in your A and B members.

Where do the A, B, and C members come from? They come from A, B, and C friends. And before we have A, B, and C friends, we have A, B, and C strangers. Where do the strangers come from? They come from our loyal members who, at some point, become promoters.

When loyal members become promoters, they refer their strangers to us. Strangers become friends through reach. If you reach enough strangers, you can turn some into friends. If you are mindful of your reputation, then friends see their values among your members and are more likely to become members themselves. And by renewing their memberships over time, members become loyal members.

And the cycle continues.

So our goal in membership development is to turn strangers into friends, friends into members, and members into loyal members—keeping in mind that there are certain things that have to happen between stages.

So what happens when we get a C member who really loves us? Well, they become a C loyal member. When a C loyal member promotes us, they bring their C friends, who are our C strangers. Those C strangers turn into our C friends, and over time turn into C members, and finally, they become C loyal members.

If there is a type of member that you're spending too many resources on, then perhaps it's time to consider pursuing a member profile that can actually help you grow. This is going to be critical because you need to be mindful of whether you're talking to an A, B, or C prospect at every stage.

A big source of membership growth comes from your existing members. If we're not paying attention to the status of our members—i.e., whether they're A, B, or C members—then we're just taking all comers, which is a dangerous thing.

My first job in membership was in the health club business twenty years ago. When I made the move to selling business memberships back in 2001, I discovered that my chamber didn't have a strategy for filtering and defining A, B, and C members. I was taught to chase each and every potential member.

The headaches caused by this lack of understanding were painful.

In *Permission Marketing*, author Seth Godin teaches that strangers become friends, friends become members, members become loyal members, and loyal members will refer their friends, who are your strangers, to your organization. Everything is going to come back to this.

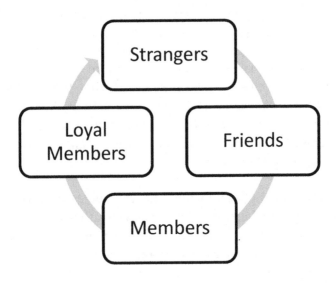

In the digital world, strangers are visitors to your website. Visitors become leads, leads turn into members, and members turn into promoters.

When the customer you should have fired becomes loyal, the downward spiral begins. Maybe that's why your membership drives aren't helping.

Buying and Justifying

People buy emotionally and they justify intellectually. For membership organizations, people join emotionally and then justify upon renewal. This means you have a year to help people justify their investments in your organization.

Connected members are engaged in your organization because you've captured their hearts. If you haven't connected with a member in the first year of membership, you'll likely lose that member for good. I interviewed businesspeople about their membership experiences for this book; as it turns out, some are willing to give you a second year, but not a third.

If members are dropping because of the improper way you sold them their memberships in the first place, then replacing a dropped member with a new one, or even two new ones, isn't going to solve your membership problem.

Consider which members stay for the long term. Go get more of those. If you can't find them, ask your long-term members where they might be.

Gravity on Top

Create a pressure that pulls people into your organization and toward higher investments over time. Incentivize and reward members for increasing their investments—not reducing them.

Think about how your organization is telling stories. Think about your marketing materials.

Make sure your marketing materials aren't just created by an awesome designer. A successful sales professional should be involved in creating the membership materials that you use to market and sell your brand. An analytical membership marketing piece will inspire fewer buying decisions. Contrastingly, an over-designed piece can over- or underwhelm a prospect.

Your prospects buy emotionally. That's how they're going to join your organization. They join emotionally and then justify their memberships intellectually upon renewal. But you only have a limited amount of time to get people acclimated to your organization before you ask them to justify their memberships by renewing for another year.

Many membership organizations complain that they have only eighty-two percent or seventy-eight percent or ninety-one percent retention rates, but these are astronomically high retention rates compared to those found in other sectors. Across all industries, we really are in a very fortunate position.

It comes down to this: If you're spending $13,000 of effort trying to chase down $8,000 of past dues, move on. Understand the economics, figure out where you went wrong in the first place, and fix that problem.

Before you get big, you've got to get good. Don't hit the gas pedal on membership growth until you understand why your existing members are there in the first place.

Surprise and Delight

My phone rang after I made a whopping $75 purchase from GoDaddy. Turns out it was Michelle from GoDaddy—calling just twenty seconds after I clicked "PAY NOW" on the GoDaddy website—to thank me for my purchase and to see how she could help me route the URLs I had just bought.

After getting over the surprise of a human response to an online purchase, I realized what a delightful experience she provided. I instantly wanted to create the same delight for my members and future members. Over the next five years, this pursuit generated nearly $100,000 in new-member revenue for the chamber.

Your future members may expect to be delighted in this way. I know, it's not as fun when they expect it, but the alternative has prospects leaving as quickly as they can type G-O-O-G-L-E.

So many online experiences trump the in-person experience, and more consumers prefer to exchange information in a digital format. Salesperson-averse shoppers are willing to give you their email addresses if it means they can satisfy their curiosity in an instant. This expectation reaches into the simplest facets of your member experience.

Your organization's brand depends on a unique experience. If you're not unique; you're easy to leave. But if you delight your members in small, subtle ways, you're easy to love.

So, as a potential future member, get the information you need from me in order to answer my questions. Do it online in a way that delights me, just as you would delight me in person.

If your organization doesn't allow me to join online, I have to wonder why.

If I can't change my own profile information in your database, you're not making it easy for me to love you.

If I can't buy more than one ticket to the mixer because you don't know if my guest is a member or not, you're making it easy to leave.

Delight your future members by creating a remarkable enrollment process on your website. If your current site or member management software can't do this, leave it and start fresh.

Quantify Your Un-Quantified Values

I met Mike Varney four years into his run at the Las Vegas Chamber of Commerce, but this story starts in Wisconsin, where Mike was the founder and CEO of Symphony Marketing before moving to Nevada to head up the marketing department of the Las Vegas Chamber of Commerce. (He is now the CEO of the chamber of commerce in Tucson, Arizona.)

Symphony Marketing was a small marketing and sales firm Mike conceived after spending two decades as a broadcast executive. In April 1997, Mike's twenty-six years of media experience collided with a membership organization. The result was a simple worksheet Mike and his team created to convert every single benefit of Las Vegas Chamber of Commerce membership into a quantified value that contributes to the return on a member's investment.

Members of the chamber get a single listing in thousands of directories printed annually. How much is that worth? Have you ever thought about it? What else do we know about the directory?

Let's just say...

- 2,000 directories are printed
- An average directory is referenced by a shopper five times per year for a buying decision
- 1,000 members are in the directory
- One-third of shoppers will buy
- An average purchase is $35 (a coffee drink is $3.50, a new car is $35,000... $35 is reasonable and conservative)
- $2,000 \times 5 \div 1,000 \div 3 \times \$35 = \$116$

A listing in your association's directory is worth $116. This exercise can be done with every benefit of your membership.

Download a worksheet at RemembershipBook.com to help you turn your memberships into quantified values.

Proactive Renewals

The West Virginia Chamber of Commerce works on renewals the hard way. They pick up the phone to touch base with each member, eventually asking permission to mail a renewal invoice for another year of membership.

It should come as no surprise that Amanda Pasdon, their director of business investment and development, spent a lot of time at the podium during a conference at which awards for innovative membership development practices were honored. The West Virginia Chamber of Commerce cleaned up.

Pasdon and President Steve Roberts have figured out that great proactive customer service yields positive changes in member retention.

To Whom Are You Referring?

The Greater Omaha Chamber of Commerce developed a referral program that allows loyal members to receive a nice perk when their friends and business associates join. Former Vice President of Small Business and Membership Jim Butler applied a discount of a full ten percent of the new member's dues to the referring member's next renewal. When Jim called me for my thoughts on his idea, I told him he was crazy, and that I was crazy enough to steal the idea.

I got a lot of these calls from Jim Butler. I suspect it's because he cut his business development teeth outside of the chamber industry. His idea wasn't a new one, but I had never seen a chamber of commerce pull it off.

The Omaha Chamber has since returned to a conventional sales team, but if your organizational overhead won't support a sales team, this is an idea worth considering.

When I started my first business in 1994, I bought a pager. (Remember those?) The paging company would put perforated sheets of business-card-sized referral cards, three or more, in my monthly statements. To refer people to the company, I just handed them one of those cards with my pager number written on it. When they eventually signed up, we both received a free month of service. I didn't pay for the paging service after the first month because of this.

AudioAcrobat.com has a similarly aggressive growth strategy. But they take the paging company's program a step further.

AudioAcrobat is an online host for audio recordings. I use it to play radio interviews, podcasts, and the like. Its best feature, in my opinion, is that it gives the user the ability to make a recording for online use from his or her phone. After you record and upload your audio files, you select a player and embed it on your website.

When you opt in for their referral program, each of your players is coded with a referral code specific to your account. Someone will play an audio file on your site and say, "Hey what is this cool little audio player thing?" When the user clicks on the player, he or she is taken to a tour of the AudioAcrobat service. If the user joins, the referring user receives a discount equal to thirty-three percent of the new user's fees for the lifetime of the subscription.

Signing up to be a referral partner is easy. You just have to click a button.

If your membership organization can find a way to implement this type of referral program, you win.

The List

The Florida Chamber of Commerce goes in with a business card and a list. They talk about their purpose, exclusively. "It's going to take four million dollars to fight sue-happy lawyers, rising workers' compensation insurance rates, and a growing anti-business sentiment in our state," they pitch. "How much are you in for? This list contains the companies that have committed $20,000 a year or more."

Most businesses, if committed to your cause, will first take note of who is on the list. Then they will notice who is missing from it. There is a certain amount of influence that goes along with this sort of subtlety.

Pulling the Deal Off the Table

When you're expected to behave as a salesperson, but you don't, you stand out. One example came when I met with a member to talk about renewing an advertising agreement.

The member was evading the purpose of the meeting, so rather than redirect the conversation as other salespeople would, I put away my advertising samples and last year's tear sheets and took out my pad of paper to take notes.

After exhausting his off-topic conversation, I explained that I would take his comments back to our staff so that his perspectives on the topics he cared about were known, and that I was sorry he wasn't ready to consider advertising.

He was shocked. As I packed up my things, he stopped me in my tracks and pulled out his checkbook.

Prospects get defensive and often feel like prey. Applicants, on the other hand, will explain why they qualify for what you offer. The chasm between the two is vast, much like the one between a two-year member and a lifetime member.

The Pain Funnel

Sandler Sales Institute's Paula Creekmore of Eugene, Oregon, says the way to engage a member is to solve his or her problems. Simple enough, right?

The pain funnel refers to a series of questions that, when asked, can help you discover the problems a member or prospect is having and how to address them. In my experience, this method results in members becoming lasting partners rather than participants.

Just like a consultant, you go into a membership meeting armed with a business card and a pad of paper, ready to take notes. There is no "membership packet," no information dump, and no folder full of flyers, programs, or menus.

You shake hands, sit down, and now what? Just ask the business owner what her top three pains are.

Pains? Yes, pains. Ask what about the business keeps her up at night.

Usually, item one is something revenue related: competition, sales, advertising, marketing, or branding. Item two is usually cost related: taxes, employment costs, human-resources management, or the rising costs of fuel and supplies. Item three is usually something specific to the industry.

If you're an industry-specific association, you can most likely respond to all three pains. For chambers of commerce, you can help with numbers one and two only.

You've written down her top three pains without giving her the opportunity to go into too much detail at this point. Now, turn your paper back to her and tell her you can help with numbers one or two. "Which would you like to talk about?"

Whichever she chooses, you're bringing her into your pain funnel by asking her to tell you more about the issue. Then, this series:

> "What have you tried?"
> "How long did it take?"
> "How much did it cost?"
> "Did it work?"

Then: "What *else* did you try? How long did it take? How much did it cost? Did it work?" And again, and again, and again, until the prospect runs out of answers.

You add up the time and money she's thrown at the problem and report back to her with the numbers. Then ask, "Are you ready to try something else?" I've never met someone who declined at this point.

These new sales habits will keep you from being put into the box labeled *salesperson*.

Qualify Your Unqualified Prospects

John Bosse is the vice president of small business for the Cincinnati USA Regional Chamber. I asked John, a veteran of twenty years with his membership organization, about how he determines who is a good prospect for his chamber.

"We look for companies with ten employees or more," he explained. John has figured out that while his chamber will sign up any business that comes to them, their bread-and-butter business members have ten or more employees. They are stable. They have specific, definable needs that his membership organization can fulfill. As a result, the Cincinnati USA Regional Chamber has a higher retention rate than most chambers of commerce its size do.

 Look at your canceled memberships. Go into records for the last three to five years to find the zip codes, employee counts, dues amounts, membership longevity, and total purchases. If you filter your data for any of one these features, you'll find some valuable information.

If you charge for dues based on employee count, sorting data by dues is too closely linked to sorting by employee count, tainting the results of this exercise. However, this is still a useful discovery tool.

How do you qualify your members? And how do you assess their dues? Are they related?

John Bosse's simple acknowledgment of his best members allows him to focus his service and retention efforts on businesses that will make the most impact on his organization.

 Study your membership to discover how many members have ten or more employees and how many have fewer. Look for other ways to group your members, depending on your specific organization. Evaluate the retention rate of each group, focusing on the first, second, and third years, and then beyond. Admit that you may be better with one kind of member over another, then prospect for the preferred business profile, and shore up your weaknesses. Make strategic changes to improve the satisfaction and loyalty of the members who are least likely to stay for long, or get rid of them altogether.

If you know your association has just a fifty percent retention rate of first-year members, imagine what you can do to your retention rate if you can increase first-year renewals by just five to ten percent.

On-Boarding

What's your on-boarding strategy when someone first becomes a member? What's your communication strategy, and how do you follow up after the sale? What happens next?

The answers to these questions will greatly determine how happy new members are in the days, weeks, and months immediately following their initial sign-up. These answers will also directly affect how many referrals you get. You can ask for a referral at the time of the membership sale but get nothing but a blank stare because for your new member, no one's coming to mind. Give your new members some time and follow up with them after the initial sale.

New members don't yet have a box in which to put your organization because they haven't had any experience with you. If you really make the on-boarding process something that delights your members, they are more likely to recommend you.

To maximize the number of referrals and testimonials with your name in them, I recommend that you attend all on-boarding programs alongside the new members you helped join.

Whether you have a member orientation or an Association 101 class, you want to give people a chance to meet each other and see that they're not alone in being new to the organization. If you sold the membership, be there to greet your members and guide them through the orientation process. Introduce them to other new members.

Pricing & Value

If Pricing Is the Chicken, Value Is the Egg

Reid Neubert and some other members were unhappy with the direction and business practices of a San Francisco professional association, so they started their own. The Council of Business Advisors is just that: an association of trusted advisors to business.

According to Neubert, council members are experienced professionals who are well regarded in their fields and have a high level of competency in their respective areas of expertise. They primarily serve executives and businesses owners and managers.

I asked Reid what caused the riff with the other organization. He said this:

"They raised their already high annual dues by fifty percent to $1,200, which we felt was much too high, and weren't sure we were getting any value added for the increase. After much consideration, I spearheaded starting our own organization, taking what we felt was most valuable from their model and brainstorming ways to make it as valuable as possible to our members."

The Price and Value of Membership

Many business structures are remarkable precisely because they are quirky or difficult. Membership organizations shouldn't be this way, in my opinion, but there are some brands that have capitalized on bizarre access strategies in the marketplace.

Starbucks recognizes that standing in line is part of the brand experience. This could be the reason behind their late adoption of drive-through windows and the limited number of cash registers, no matter how large the café.

Wireless phone companies make exclusive deals with service providers in order to get the most marketing exposure for their premium products.

Sure, Apple could have sold more iPhones by cutting deals with both AT&T and Verizon upon launching, but only it was only AT&T that agreed to the terms Apple demanded—that is, until Verizon inked a deal with Apple two years later.

In this case, difficulty and complexity are written into the business plan.

As complicated as it is to do business with companies like these ones, they are hoping—no, not hoping, *banking*—that they will keep you longer because of it.

Wireless companies know it is a hassle to change. Starbucks knows that waiting is inconvenient, but the customers they attract don't mind being seen in line at Starbucks. Some brand experts argue that Starbucks customers *want to be seen in line* at Starbucks.

Many online service providers know that if they charge a monthly service fee, you will weigh the hassle of cancelling against the low cost of the service (even if it's a service you don't use enough to justify paying for it). This is called a *painless price point.*

In my five years at Gold's Gym, we weren't this way. Other franchises in urban centers would charge a ridiculously low amount, say, $19 per month, in the hopes that customers would keep the membership months or years longer than needed instead of initiating the cancellation process.

About two-thirds of chambers of commerce charge dues based on how many people are employed by each member's business. You tell them how many employees your business has and they tell you how much your dues will be. It's called "fair share" dues. I've never liked this system.

This is a lazy way to build a business or membership organization. Members who pay $1,000 per year are getting the same benefits as the member who pays $300 is.

Whoever came up with this strategy surely was not a large employer, and possibly not a capitalist.

In a sluggish economy, consumers re-evaluate the value proposition of their business relationships. In April 2008, as gas prices nearly doubled within a month, retailers complained that consumers stopped spending money when, in fact, they were simply adjusting personal budgets.

At about that same time, the Salem Chamber was in its second year of a membership structure which allowed members to choose their investment level, and boy were we glad. We called it value-based tiers.

As businesses were adjusting to their customers' adjustment, they made a little extra time to wheel and deal with their vendors. The twelve months following the fuel price-doubling would prove to be a historic economic crisis for Americans.

Michael Dalby, then-CEO of One Southern Indiana, once told me he is "the poster child for changing to tiered dues in a down economy."

One Southern Indiana initiated their tiered dues program as the financial meltdown swept the country. A year later, the organization had fewer members and more revenue.

It hardly seems possible. Even after business closures caused an unusually high number of lost members, membership organizations have gained in membership revenue by offering their members a choice in investment, a choice in value, and a choice in status.

Businesses that offer more value for higher investments will most easily appreciate the strategy behind membership tiers.

Bundling Rewards Members and Organizations Both

"I once was charged more at the drive-through because I was driving a bigger car," said no person, ever. Membership organizations that assess dues based on the number of employees each member has often find that they are leaving money on the table and member satisfaction at the door.

Open-membership organizations that hope to grow in revenue can benefit their members—and their bottom lines—by offering packages. Properly constructed bundles benefit both buyer and seller.

My guideline: three hundred members or fewer, start with three levels; five hundred or more, use five. If you're in between, you can thumb wrestle for it.

There are two different types of tiered pricing:
- Good-better-best
- Ascension

Good-better-best works best for small, closed or consumer-focused organizations. I mention closed organizations because some associations are invitation only and have very different value propositions than open organizations do.

Ascension pricing levels are very different. Where good-better-best models address the same or similar need of a consumer, ascension pricing recognizes the different needs of a varied audience.

Take American Express cards and benefits, for example. Joining American Express begins with selecting from four categories of cards: personal, small business, corporate or pre-paid. Within each of these categories are options that look a lot like good-better-best models. The corporate card has six options, while the others each have three.

To build an effective ascending-tier schedule, you must first create a solid, systematic approach to member segmentation. Getting this right will create a clear path to building value for specific member profiles.

Allow Members to Choose Their Own Investments

As someone who coaches business membership organizations through the conversion from the (un)fair-share model to the value-based tier model, I repeatedly get asked the same questions about tiers. Here they are for your consideration.

We're concerned that too many of our members are too small for tiers.

Membership options work *because* of small business, not in spite of them. Now your smallest members can play with the big kids, if they choose to. Business owners have needs and expectations. Allowing them to buy at a level that matches their preference is capitalism at its finest.

Can an organization be too small for tiers?

I don't believe so. This model transcends size, scope, or territory.

Why would we switch to tiers?

Well for one, if you use a fair-share model now, you are punishing your members for growing and rewarding them for lying to you. Neither of these are a good premise for a long-lasting relationship. Plus, your members are already doing business this way, just not with you. Fast food restaurants, cable and satellite television companies, health clubs... They all use tiered packaging in some way. This isn't new; it's just new to associations.

How do we prevent large investors from reducing their investments?

First, build an incredible bundle of benefits that rewards a higher level of investment. Then use what I call the "reverse-employee-count safety net," in which large employers are not eligible for lower memberships. This is a great transition from fair-share models. The key here is to put this in the fine print so that it's not a starting point, just a safety net. Hence the name.

Do tiers still feature a fair-share component?

They certainly could, but I don't believe they should (other than the safety net). It's important to get buy-in from your members in free-market fashion. The safety net is used in a purchase transaction, not in the needs analysis and selection processes.

Can tiers be customized?

Customized, yes. Have replaceable/interchangeable benefits, probably not. From associations to chambers of commerce, no tiered membership plans will be exactly the same. (If there are, you haven't considered the uniqueness of your membership.) Members should be encouraged to customize their membership. In sales terms, this might be considered *upselling*.

Most packages are a starting point from which you create a customized plan for servicing a member or client. *"I'll have a number two, super-sized, with a Coke."* Through some very simple marketing and sales techniques, your marketing materials can reflect the customizable nature of tiers, encouraging members to make each package their own.

Where do we begin?

First, make a list of all the benefits you offer members for their dues.

Second, add on the features of your organization for which you charge members. This includes business services, advertising tickets and ticket packages, subscriptions, programs, trainings, and so forth. (Don't include event sponsorships for this exercise.) Put an X next to any of these items that are limited in supply or sell out. We're not going to use these just yet.

Third, quantify the value of each feature using a reasonable conversion rate and average sale. (See *Quantify Your Un-Quantified Values* on page eighty-seven.) Start moving these benefits into packages with your members in mind, and you're well on your way.

How do we get our board onboard?

Remember that your board consists of members. They want more value, too. Tiers will do two things for you: raise revenue and increase value. Which are they more resistant to? Price increases. Focus on how tiers will improve the value for members. Many organizations have gone the other way, causing the proposal to be rejected by the board. If you can't get your board excited about this idea, it's because you've focused on what's easy. Raising the value is hard.

Should we be selling from low to high or high to low?

I learned this lesson the hard way when I realized I was selling the high-priced membership tier from the back of the brochure to a member who was a legitimate prospect for the highest tier. Big spenders prefer to buy from the front of the catalog, not the back.

There is a reason grocery stores put the milk in the back of the store; it's so you have to walk through the other stuff to get there, being tempted by both on the way there and on the way back. Simple staple item: milk. It's just like your simple staple item: the basic membership. To get there, you're going to tempt your prospects along the way.

So, sell high-to-low. Make the prospect see and consider all of the things that they will be passing up by selecting a lower tier. At the very least, they'll have a better understanding of what your organization actually does.

How do we track the delivery of benefits?

Tracking will be required for deliverables that operate as their own businesses within your organization so that revenue and expenses associated with these programs are not misappropriated to a membership line item in your budget.

The problem, as I see it, is that your organization may not have been accountable for service delivery in the past. You could use vouchers or a coupon book as a delivery and tracking mechanism, but by themselves, they do not have a personal service component desired by higher investors.

In all my research, I haven't found any reproducible system for tracking, so I created one. It's a simple matrix system, really, but most associations would prefer to automate this process.

If your database or customer relationship management (CRM) system allows you to cluster benefits while tracking them independently, then you have the capability to automate tracking. Many membership management software companies offer this functionality and at least three of them check in with me when they have updates and would like some feedback.

Should we upgrade members throughout the year or upon renewal?

Both are needed for a successful conversion to a tiered model. If you're on an anniversary renewal program, pull out members you'd like to visit about two or three months prior to their renewal date and hand-deliver the renewal invoice with the new tier options listed— but note that only the higher tiers should be displayed. They've demonstrated that you're worth what they have been investing in, so don't give them the option to downgrade their investment unless the other option is losing them as a member.

What will tiers do for sales and retention?

Converting to tiers is not a solution to your sales or retention problem. However, some associations report higher new-member revenue due to members having a choice in tier selection instead being forced to give a simple yes or no to a sales pitch.

Most organizations see a higher dues-per-member average. At the Salem Area Chamber of Commerce, average annual dues were up twenty-five percent after less than two years, and new member revenue was up nearly twenty percent after just one year.

One of the subtleties of a successful tiered dues plan can be found in the pricing. After researching my own membership drops, I found that retention increased dramatically for members investing more than $500 per year. It's no coincidence that the next membership level was priced above this threshold at $650. This move allows an organization to focus retention efforts in accordance with its priorities.

You might think it's obvious to focus your retention efforts on members investing less than $500 per year, but simple math suggests that, given Member A is investing $325 and Member B is investing $650, your efforts to retain Member B will yield twice the results for the same effort.

We currently have a salesperson who is paid a salary and a commission for new sales and has an incentive for renewing memberships. Are there any recommendations/tips for management regarding sales personnel while the restructuring of dues is occurring?

As someone who once made his living in membership sales, I can tell you that you never need to fire a salesperson as long as you can just change his or her commission structure. The more a salesperson's compensation relies on commission, the more stress you'll cause by changing it.

On occasion, changing sales compensation is necessary for the long-term success of your pricing structure, but it's not often that I recommend it.

What would we do with our Chairman's Circle program?

Many business-focused membership organizations have a premium membership such as a Chairman's Circle or a Trustees Membership. In most cases, this level can be easily blended into your new tiers. For example, it could become your highest or second-highest tier, depending on price, value, market, and number of members.

How do we assign a dollar value to membership levels?

Use formulas used by media ad buyers and IEG (sponsorship.com) for accuracy, and then pair that with conservative numbers of impressions for realistic values you can take to the bank. The quantification worksheets mentioned on page eighty-nine in this book will be of great help. Get them online at RemembershipBook.com.

Our staff and board members are concerned about taking away benefits that members have been receiving for years.

I don't endorse taking away any benefits. Your current benefits will be your basic business tier. This obviously puts pressure on your organization to add benefits to complete your marketable packages. That's where someone like me comes in. You and your staff may not have the time or experience to do the necessary research I've acquired since 2004.

Will members who don't upgrade feel less important?

The point here is to put a higher value on your devalued organization. Price is an important component of value. The question, therefore, really is "Why do you let these businesses devalue your organization by investing less than it costs to serve them?"

By investing at the minimum level, below your cost-per-member benchmark, are members not telling you that they should be less important to you? That they aren't committed to your cause? That they won't be around long enough for you to take notice?

I am concerned that the outcome would be a prescribed range of membership benefits and that the flexibility we have had in the past will drop away. How do we retain flexibility for members to participate in ways that are best

for them and avoid a limited, prescribed cafeteria plan?

The old way wouldn't go away, but you would "overlay" a new, ascending, tiered pricing structure on your existing schedule, which will be based on value instead of how many employees members have, or say they have. Many (though not all) members want a prescribed set of benefits to cure their ills.

If you're looking for a marketing advantage, we have a membership for that. If you want a higher level of involvement, we have a membership for that, and if you want to support the chamber's work without any involvement, we have a membership for that, too.

These memberships should speak to specific needs, which is a great improvement over the current scenario. Flexibility is enhanced—not limited—by a tiered structure.

One concern is that my organization may end up being stuck and won't see any value-added benefit of joining a crowd when we want to make sure our message is heard. If we transition from one to three sponsors per event to many more, how do we make sure the messages don't drown out each other?

The goal is to create a membership structure that scales, which means you need to be able to sell five, fifty, or five hundred of them. If you can't accommodate these numbers with any single benefit, then that benefit cannot be included in the tiers. You will use what your organization already offers to create packages, but sponsorships are not included in tiers because you can't sell fifty of the same sponsorship. The value wouldn't be there, and it would lose its desirability.

I don't want a new structure to result in the organization being stuck providing services that are great today but "not so much" tomorrow. How do we avoid this trap?

The feedback loop can be created whether or not you have tiered pricing, and this new membership structure is as fluid and dynamic as you need it to be. Best practices in membership organizations suggest that staff should be reviewing and adjusting the new structure annually. Changes can be made according to usage of individual features or based on trends in your industry or market niche.

If this is revenue neutral, how do you keep a resource-intensive dues methodology from driving up costs and tipping the apple cart over?

This plan shouldn't be revenue neutral, but it leans toward overhead neutral. Early in the process, quantify the variable costs of benefits you would like to include in the tiers so that there are no surprises. Tracking should be done by staff and isn't optional, but not every service needs to be accounted for from a financial or delivery standpoint.

Find your cost-per-member benchmark. This is what it costs you to do what you do for each member annually. Total revenue minus any grants or government contracts divided by the number of members equals your cost per member. (Some experts recommend removing all program revenue, as well. I leave it in under the assumption that your programs fit your mission and function.)

Don't think for a moment that I'm casting aside the membership model. The default business plan of a membership organization requires that many paying members offset the costs incurred by the high-needs members.

This does not take into account the power of choice. When given a choice, a portion of your membership will choose a higher level. If you price your tiers correctly for your organization and market, this portion of members can bring about an increase in revenue.

When I was in the health club business, we had great concern that two members, side by side on a treadmill, would get to talking about how much they each paid in membership dues. If one had a corporate rate, the other might feel like his or her membership at the club wasn't worth the cost. That type of pricing is often mistakenly called "promotional pricing." It should be called "de-motional pricing." Lowering prices, couponing, and discounting is not a promotion if it lowers your value in the eyes of the consumer.

Put a new price on the value of your association by creating clear levels of service. One effect of having these tiers is that when a person feels he or she isn't getting the right level of service or benefits, the solution is as simple as matching the person with the right membership.

Tiers Round Up

Make no mistake: this is a new way of thinking for your old-school membership organization. Adding a premium price for status hasn't been talked about since associations started adding in Chairman's Circles. This is the first step. Now build the rest of the rungs for the ladder that can take any business from the bottom to the top.

My answers to these questions may seem blunt at times, but I have the benefit of learning by doing. Through my own association's conversion process, I was the graphic designer who designed the award-winning marketing materials, the salesman who tested the packages, the researcher who sought out the best and worst in my industry, and the marketer who planned and executed the launch and collateral. Since then, I've done the same things for countless membership organizations.

Go

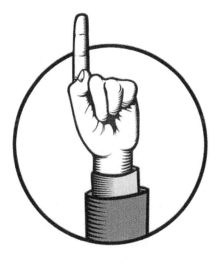

Question Your Answers

Put associations from different regions and markets in a room and the questions begin: How many members do you have? What is your retention rate? Is that in dollars or number of members? What is your turnover? What is your conversion rate?

Stephanie Kirksey says if you want new answers, ask new questions. Kirksey is the former executive vice president of the Greater Richmond (VA) Chamber of Commerce and a co-conspirator in my quest to change membership development strategies among membership organizations.

As chair of the membership development division of the Association of Chamber of Commerce Executives, Kirksey wrote a newsletter column that suggests we ask questions like these: *Who are our members? Do we have the "right" members? Are our members engaged? Are we spending all of our time on the members that offer the least or the most financial opportunity to the organization? Do the bigger/key companies find clear value in the chamber? Do members know how to optimize their memberships?*

In an article published by the Western Association of Chamber Executives, Nancy Hoffman Vanyek challenges associations to update their business model or face the Uber alternative. Nancy is CEO of the Greater San Fernando Valley (CA) Chamber.

"It's become clear that taxi cab companies are struggling to keep up with what the consumer wants and with what Uber delivers on," she wrote. "Instead of changing their model, taxi cabs want to eliminate the other model altogether or at the very least make it conform so that taxi cabs are not displaced.

"Are we doing the same thing in our chambers?"

Have More Bad Ideas

Many associations are lemurs. Most chambers of commerce certainly are, as well. They follow the leader. They copy the map of any program with results, regardless of the relative impact on their own customer base.

While it's fine to copy what is working somewhere else, you have relied on your counterparts to ask their own members that same question, devise an answer, and hope they share the results with you.

The problem is that by relying too heavily on other organizations, you're being too safe. Put in a different way, if you want to be known as a resource that helps your members find solutions, then solve something. Take a risk. Fail at something new. At least you'll have tried, and hopefully what you failed at was something designed to solve a problem your members actually have.

I've failed plenty of times offering new things to my members. There are two noteworthy points about failure: One, members don't remember your failures as much as they remember your successes, and two, you learn something from each failure that makes yours a more valuable organization.

To have more good ideas, start generating more bad ideas. If it's a numbers game, the good ones are in there. The challenge is in knowing the difference— that's the "art," as Godin explains in *Linchpin*.

Expectations Have Changed

Perhaps the best reason for the existence of this book is that the nature of your membership organization hasn't kept up with consumer expectations. The proliferation of things like social networks, online banking, paperless statements, and a Wikipedia world has transformed behaviors and forever set new expectations for your organization.

It's not hard to find reasons to satisfy these expectations. They lead to greater revenue, deeper customer knowledge, better efficiency and leaner organizations.

Social networks have lowered the cost of connecting people to zero. The once-high barriers between an organization and a customer have since been knocked down. Join an organization and pay its dues, wear your business clothes to a networking event, and start working the pond. (Tip of the hat to Darcy Rezac, Gayle Rezac, and Judy Thompson, authors of *Work the Pond*, a great book about how, why, and where to build relationships.)

Thanks to Facebook, LinkedIn, and thousands of other social networks, you don't have to join anything, pay anything, or even get dressed in the morning to find prospects and potential partners.

What these technologies don't do as well, however, is build trusting relationships. If you're concerned that social networks are encroaching on your space, remember that you can create a culture that not only encourages relationships, but instigates them, too. Your culture can't necessarily be recreated on the Internet. If it can, that's a different problem.

It's important to note that an online world gives a voice to the lazy and socially unskilled, where previously a cultural filter kept them from participating. If people want only to take from the pool, maybe it's better that they do so online instead of within your organization.

These sharks will scare away the big fish. More than ever before, your members value peer-to-peer connections. If you ignore this fact, don't be surprised when your connection events are overrun by salespeople, each of them trying to sell to the others.

"Peer" has become a much more specific target than it used to be. Separating your members into peer groups could be the best decision you've ever made.

When you chase new revenue by lowering your price point and offering monthly memberships or and short-term trials, you are inviting this potentially negative element into your membership organization. I think it's fine to explore these options, but do so with that critical truth in mind.

Never betray your crew by inviting the pirates aboard your ship.

Build a Better Mousetrap

How do financial institutions engage with their customers? The answer to this question and conversations on this topic can offer a trail of clues you can use to improve your membership organization.

In their book *Made to Stick*, authors Chip Heath and Dan Heath explore what makes some ideas last while others die. They share the story of an unnamed bank that's in the process of evaluating whether to invest more in online services for its customers. At the time, ten percent of the bank's customers logged in to their accounts online.

At first glance, this data doesn't set up a good argument for investing in more online services, so it's a good thing the bank dug deeper to find out more about their customers.

The bank discovered that this small sector of their customer base—this ten percent—actually represented seventy percent of monthly deposits. This singular finding was pure gold for the bank's business plan.

By identifying this common thread among its ideal customer, the bank could build a better mousetrap to attract more of the same.

Roles, Goals, and Why

I've been surrounded by amazing teachers my whole life. One of them was a real estate developer named Richard V. Hatten who taught me not to be a five-goaler.

"What's a five-goaler?" I once asked him.

"A five-goaler," he explained, "has five goals. Their first goal is the first break, their second goal is lunch, their third goal is their second break, their fourth goal is quitting time, and their fifth goal is payday."

I was nineteen when I learned what not to be. It would take me another decade to be able to put into words what I did want to be, and why. My "why" didn't include breaks.

Sales expert Chip Eichelberger teaches that we need a constant visual reminder of our "why." He keeps his in the shower. (It's laminated.) Mine is on my bathroom mirror and in my office next to my desk.

It lists the roles I play throughout my day. Each role is a reminder that someone is depending on me for something valuable.

It also lists my goals—personal ones like camping vacations with my son and financial ones like seeing a certain number in my retirement account.

Then there's the "why."

I learned that there's a direct correlation between job creation and a child's quality of life. When jobs are created, in your community or mine, a child with two unemployed parents becomes a child with employed parents. The opportunities for this child are exponentially greater because of those jobs.

If you're doing business in Salem, we're working for you. That was my mantra while working in membership development for the Salem Area Chamber of Commerce for eleven years. The work we did saved jobs, created jobs, and made dreams come true for entrepreneurs and aspiring employees alike.

Today, I get to do this work through you. I love your success stories. When you make more money, your membership organization makes more money. When you get a sale, it's because you are solving business problems in your region, industry, or profession. When you solve common business problems, you're improving the health of a business, which saves jobs or creates them.

Raise Your Hand

If you don't tell your story, they will make one up about you. The stories of your membership organization are being told by your members or by former members you have failed.

Clinging to yesterday's agenda is killing your organization's future, little by little. The longer you take to make a change, the greater the risk of having a United Airlines moment, all caused by an antiquated value proposition.

The remarkable nature of your membership organization lies within the stories your members tell about why they joined and why they continue to stand with your organization.

I refuse to sit and wish for more media, more attention, or more advertising dollars. Refuse with me. The clock is ticking.

This manifesto exists because I'm seeking people who want to shake things up with me. People like Adam Legge, Sherry Taylor, Aaron Nelson, April Bragg, Matt McCormick and Paul Farmer.

What got you here won't get you there. Tell a new story for your organization. Put your members in your story. Act like their agent, because you are.

If you find that you are worried about the future of your organization, perhaps it is because you are not doing anything about it.

The story of your remarkable membership organization starts today. Let's re-membership. Raise your hand and point your finger. Let's go.

About the Author

Photo by AJ Coots

Kyle Sexton is an award-winning marketing strategist and international speaker and is the author of several books on the topics of membership development, marketing, and innovation. He was recognized in 2011 by *Chamber Executive* magazine as one of the most influential innovators in the chamber of commerce industry.

Kyle is the chamber industry's foremost authority on membership tiers, and he guides organizations through the transition from a traditional dues method to value-based tiers. His research and methods have been featured in industry publications as well as at national conventions and regional conferences.

Formerly the director of business development for the Salem Area Chamber of Commerce, Kyle was recognized as the 2007 Chamber Staff Person of the Year by the Western Association of Chamber Executives. His innovations have been featured in *The Wall Street Journal*. Kyle's pioneering "Face2Face" platform on SalemChamber.org propelled the site to become the top-ranked local or regional chamber of commerce site on the web, as measured by Alexa.com.

In 2008, he created what is now ChamberPeople.com, the web's largest free social network exclusive to chambers of commerce. He is also the creator of the Member SalesEngine, an automated online membership sales module and lead-generation tool for chambers of commerce.

Kyle is a faculty member for the Institute of Organizational Management since 2008, located at these universities:

- University of Arizona
- Loyola Marymount University
- Villanova University
- University of Wisconsin
- University of Georgia

He leads courses on:

- Marketing strategies
- Strategic communications
- Integrating strategic technology solutions
- Tech trends and tools
- Sponsorship solicitation
- Communicating through the media

With over one thousand memberships sold, Kyle received the Lifetime Achievement Award from the Association of Chamber of Commerce Executives Circle of Champions sales division.

He has been marketing and selling memberships since 1996. Prior to working for chambers of commerce, he was the director of marketing and corporate services for a chain of Gold's Gym locations in western Oregon. He earned the 2001 Gold's Gym International Award for Outstanding Advertising, for which candidates from six hundred franchises worldwide were considered.

Kyle received the 1994 Pioneer Award for his first business venture, a College Pro Home Painters franchise, which he operated for two years while attending the University of Oregon.

Kyle plays a little guitar and lives in Salem, Oregon, with his son, Wyatt.

Acknowledgements

So many thanks. To **Mom** for your eternal support and encouragement. To my brothers, **Britt** and **Troy**, for being so disciplined and for showing me the way. To **Dad** for planting business in my head when I was twelve.

To my other family members and my teammates at the **Salem Area Chamber of Commerce**: Sharron Seideman, Rita Rasmussen, Carole Reynolds, Cori Pratt, Jason Brandt, Kathy Moore, Jessica Chambers, Tonya Valentine, Chandra Andersen, Lisa Franceschi-Campbell, Kim Leighty, Tracey Etzel, Susie Ingersoll, Chris McLaran, Sylvia Forster, and Myron Musick. You inspire me and keep me grounded. All-stars, every single one of you.

To **Mike Varney** for challenging my reality. To **Shane Moody** for being untouchable and accessible at the same time. To **Troy McLellan** for keeping me focused when I was frustrated. To **Matt Pivarnik** for setting the bar even higher right before it was my turn to jump. To **Doug Holman** for always speaking the truth about this business and for being great at what you do. To **Ben Wolf** for participating in my brainstorm sessions. To **Kate Volman** for the phone calls you thought were just for you. To **Amanda Pasdon** for your endless encouragement. To **Dawn Moliterno** for helping me make sense of pricing. To **Steve Millard** for pushing the industry and wearing more hats than I thought possible.

To **Mick Fleming** for your steady hand and voice. To **Dave Kilby** for having high standards and forcing me to keep my research fresh. To **Ray Langen** for sharing your love for the people side of this business. To **Keith Woods** for showing me that research can be fun. To **Paula Creekmore** for the sales training I use nearly every day, even in non-sales endeavors. To **Cameron Herold** for six months of business training that will last a lifetime. To **Alan Corder** for giving me a shot.

To the late **Mike McLaran** for your hunch on hiring day.

To **Jennifer Powers** and **Tim Fahndrich** for fifty-two Thursday afternoons. To the late **Shaun Lumachi** for pushing constantly. To **Tom Hoffert** for that one day when you were the difference, and every day since.

To **Scott Juranek** and the folks at Micronet, makers of ChamberMaster and MemberZone member management software, for your belief in my work and support of the message.

And to **Seth Godin** for helping me find my voice and putting into plain English what had been on the tip of my tongue for years.

Bibliography

These are the books that inspired this work or are referenced within it. Some are just ones that you should read. They're listed here in no particular order.

Linchpin: Are You Indispensable? by Seth Godin
Godin describes this book as his life's work, and it scared the hell out of me when he said it would be his last book. Thankfully, what he meant is that it was to be his last book from a traditional publisher. *Linchpin* describes the traits required in order to get away from being a replaceable cog in someone else's system and moving into the artful work that matters.

Made to Stick by Chip Heath and Dan Heath
The Heath brothers do their homework. The revelations I had while reading this book really helped me to understand why my strategies and practices work.

The Purple Cow by Seth Godin
I've had more people thank me for recommending this book than any other. If you want to know how to move away from conventional advertising and turn your business into pure marketing, read this book.

Little Teal Book of Trust: How to Earn It, Grow It, and Keep It to Become a Trusted Advisor in Sales, Business & Life by Jeffrey Gitomer
Whether you've lost it or you're looking to keep it, Jeffrey simplifies a very tender topic. To put trust into business terms is invaluable.

Poke the Box by Seth Godin
This is the first book from Godin's Domino Project, a mostly digital publishing venture with Amazon. Brilliant. I highlighted more lines in this work than any other, ever.

How to Nail Voice Mail by Shawna Schuh
Shawna teaches you how to behave like someone who wants to be invited back to dinner—or to a dinner meeting. It's not just about voicemail; it's about business communications.

Tribes: We Need You to Lead Us by Seth Godin
You can probably insert the name of your membership organization each time Godin uses the word *tribes* in this work.

Double Double: How to Double Your Revenue and Profit in 3 Years or Less by Cameron Herold
Cameron was one of my first business mentors. Reading this book was like reading my own mind—probably because he put all of these ideas in there in the first place.

Permission Marketing: Turning Strangers into Friends, and Friends into Customers by Seth Godin
This map about email marketing still works seventeen years after it was written. Read it and apply it to social media and a million other places where we give or ask for permission.

Getting Things Done: The Art of Stress-Free Productivity by David Allen
No-nonsense advice to help you become more productive. I wonder if my book could have been completed without David's.

Oh, Shift! How to Change Your Life with One Little Letter by Jennifer Powers
You could read this book at a poetry jam and win the crowd and the crown. Jennifer's raw and real style makes for a beautiful read.

The Dip: A Little Book That Teaches You When to Quit (and When to Stick) by Seth Godin
My least favorite of Godin's books, but only because of what it exposed in me. *The Dip* is all about work... you know, the hard part. I learned a lot—like that sometimes, quitting is winning.

Can I Have 5 Minutes of Your Time by Hal Becker
I met Hal in Toronto in 2001, and his sales philosophy became my marketing philosophy: "I'm independently wealthy and I don't need your business." Have confidence in your business strategy. I love Hal's work.

Go For No! Yes Is the Destination, No Is How You Get There by Richard Fenton and Andrea Waltz
In a world inundated with books on techniques for getting to yes, Richard Fenton and Andrea Waltz recommend just the opposite. Andrea and Richard are knowledgeable and inspiring.

Made in the USA
Monee, IL
12 July 2020